Easy As Pie Bookkeeping For Itty Bitty® Businesses

Organize You Book & Records for Business Success

No matter how small your business is you are required to keep books and records. Beyond that requirement, knowing your numbers is key to success and this book will show you how to accomplish that.

In this revolutionary Itty Bitty® Book, Joe DiChiara shows you how to organize your business transactions into a set of books and records that track your business finances easily and effortlessly.

For example, you will learn:

- What bookkeeping is.
- Why you need bookkeeping.
- How to create an awesome paperless file system.
- How to create your chart of accounts, the backbone of your bookkeeping system.
- Understanding your role and your accountant's role in the bookkeeping process.

If you are interested in an easy-to-read, easy-to-follow basic bookkeeping system, pick up a copy of this powerful little book today.

Your Amazing Itty Bitty® Personal Bookkeeping Book

15 Simple Steps To Learning How To Do Your Own Bookkeeping In Less Than A Day

Joe DiChiara
CPA/Business Consultant

Published by Itty Bitty® Publishing
A subsidiary of S & P Productions, Inc.

Printed in the United States of America

Itty Bitty® Publishing
311 Main Street, Suite D
El Segundo, CA 90245
(310) 640-8885

ISBN: 978-1-931191-91-3

This book is dedicated to my 4 children Anthony, Frankie, Jackie and Winston.

Stop by our Itty Bitty® website to find interesting blog entries regarding your personal bookkeeping system.

www.IttyBittyPublishing.com
Or contact me at

BEDROCK
BUSINESS BUILDERS
www.**bedrockbusinessbuilders**.com

Table of Contents

Introduction

This itty bitty book is intended for individuals that are either thinking about starting a business, recently started a business or have been operating a small business and never really got a handle on their bookkeeping. Reading this book will provide you with the following:

1. A basic understanding of what bookkeeping is; why it's needed and how it's done.
2. Simple step by step instructions on creating your own set of books and records.
3. An understanding of the role you and your accountant should be taking in the bookkeeping process.
4. The knowledge of how to "Know Your Numbers". One of the keys to financial success.
5. A better understanding of the fundamentals of small business.
6. Financial Knowledge and Empowerment.

Step 1
Why You Need Bookkeeping

It's every business owner's legal requirement to maintain "books and records" and bookkeeping is the main process used to create them. A good bookkeeping system will enable you to produce timely financial information that will help you operate more efficiently and hopefully more profitably.

1. Read IRS Publication 583 Starting A Business and Keeping Records. https://www.irs.gov/pub/irs-pdf/p583.pdf
2. Understand that financial knowledge is financial power.
3. Remove any of the fears and doubts that may be blocking you from addressing the financial aspect of your business.
4. Take full responsibility for the bookkeeping process and ultimate financial condition of your business.
5. Know your end game by reviewing tax returns and financial reports that are generated from your bookkeeping process.

Why You Need Bookkeeping

- Maintaining books and records is a legal requirement.
- Proper bookkeeping will help you make sound business decisions.
- As a business owner you are ultimately responsible for keeping your books and records.
- Your books and records must clearly reflect what has been reported on your tax returns.
- When you sign your tax return you are attesting under penalties of perjury that all of the information included on the return is true, accurate and complete.
- Know and understand your financial end game.

Step 2
What Bookkeeping Is

Bookkeeping is a process designed to compile business transactions into a set of organized financial reports.

1. Understand that each and every transactions conducted in your business must be reported on your tax return.
2. Identify the 6 key transaction components needed to record each transaction:
    a. Date
    b. Amount
    c. Payee/Payer
    d. Category
    e. Account
    f. Description
3. Think of the process that will be required to insert the transaction information into your financial reports and tax return.
4. Identify where the transactions will be reported on your financial reports and tax returns.

What Bookkeeping Is

- Bookkeeping is a business process.
- Bookkeeping connects your transactions and original documents to your financial reports and tax returns.
- Your books and records tell the documented story of your business and bookkeeping helps put it in order.
- Bookkeeping is the step before accounting.
- Every business transaction must go through the bookkeeping process.

Step 3
Determine Your Bookkeeping Objectives

Producing an accurate Balance Sheet and Income Statement is the ultimate purpose in the bookkeeping process. There are many facets to bookkeeping and how it occurs. Determining exactly what your short term and long term objectives are will be essential in deciding what role you take on when doing your own bookkeeping.

1. Meet with your accountant and determine what reports are needed and when.
2. Determine if you need real time, monthly, quarterly or an annual accounting of your transactions.
3. Create a list of goals and financial benchmarks for your business.
4. Determine what information you need to compare your results against your goals.
5. Learn about the Balance Sheet and Income Statement, your key financial reports.

Determine Your Bookkeeping Objectives

- A strong bookkeeping system is essential in producing key financial reports and information about your business.
- Your key financial reports are the Balance Sheet and Income Statement.
- The Balance Sheet is a snapshot of the financial status of your business.
- There are three main sections of a Balance Sheet: Assets, Liabilities and Equity.
- Assets & Liabilities are segregated into current and long term.
- Current is due or payable in less than one year and Long Term is due or payable in more than one year.
- The Income Statement shows the results of your operations for a specific time period.
- There are two main sections of an Income Statement:
    - Revenue
    - Expenses

Step 4
Working With Your Accountant

You must retain the services of a good proactive small business accountant experienced in working with startups and businesses. Your accountant should work with you throughout the year opposed to meeting you once a year at tax time.

1. If you have an accountant determine if he or she can provide the hands on guidance needed to create a good bookkeeping system with appropriate oversight.
2. If you need to find a new accountant create a profile of the type of person you would like to work with.
3. Interview a few accountants and determine if they provide the kind of hands on guidance you need to keep a solid set of books and records.
4. Ask your bank manager to refer a good small business accountant.

Working With Your Accountant

- You need a pro-active accountant to help guide you and your business.
- A proactive accountant will assist you in creating a solid bookkeeping system.
- Stick with a sole practitioner or small accounting firm. Many larger accounting firms will assign small business accounts to inexperienced staff members.
- Proper tax and business planning is a year round event, not to be conducted during tax preparation time.
- Take careful steps to retain the right accountant for you and your business.
- Find an accountant that is organized and will provide close personal attention.

Step 5
The Role You Play In Bookkeeping

Careful consideration must be made when deciding on your role in the bookkeeping process.

1. Review the volume and complexity of the transactions that need to be recorded.
2. Make an honest assessment of your skill set and determine what aspects of the bookkeeping process you should handle directly.
3. Determine the value of your time and compare it to the cost of hiring or having someone else do it.
4. Segregate the bookkeeping tasks, such as data entry and record keeping for easy delegation.
5. Delegate those functions to staff or individuals in the best strategic position to complete the task efficiently. IE: Have the individual spending petty cash organize the receipts and fill out a petty cash report.

When You Should Do Your Own Bookkeeping

- Doing your own bookkeeping does not mean doing it alone.
- It's easy to segregate bookkeeping tasks into record keeping, filing, data entry, reconciliations, review and oversight, etc.
- You do not have to handle all of the bookkeeping task, only the ones that make financial sense taking your time into account.
- You should never be completely hands off when it comes to the bookkeeping process.
- Bookkeeping is a team effort.

Step 6
Create Your Chart of Accounts

Your chart of accounts is the backbone of your bookkeeping system. The chart will list the categories and subcategories in the same order they appear in your financial statements.

1. Create a list of all of the categories and subcategories as they appear on your Balance Sheet and Income Statement.
2. Create an organized numbering system assigned to each category and subcategory to further organize your chart.
3. Leave sufficient gaps between the numbers to allow for additional categories.

Create Your Chart of Accounts.

- Sidestepping the chart of accounts will lead to sloppy, inefficient financial reports.
- Your chart needs to be well organized.
- Structure your chart in a way to provide the information as you & your accountant need to review it on your financial reports. For example:
    - Insurance
        - Auto
        - Truck
        - Liability
        - Umbrella
    - Professional Fees
        - Accounting
        - Legal

Step 7
Create Your Transactions Processes

Your transaction processes are the steps taken to consummate a transaction from start to finish. Capturing and recording the information from those transactions is called a bookkeeping process. Make a list of each type of transaction you will conduct.

1. For each type of transaction list the following information:
    a. Who initiates it?
    b. Where does it take place?
    c. How is it documented?
    d. Who obtains the document?
    e. Where is the document sent to be recorded?
    f. Who records the transaction?
    g. Who files the document?
    h. Where and how is it filed?
2. Review the list with your accountant and determine what your bookkeeping processes will be.
3. Create an item mapping listing which category each transaction will be posted to. IE: Staples-Office Supplies, Hess-Auto: Gas, XYZ Realty-Rent.

Create Your Transactions Processes

- A documented transaction process is your bookkeeping instruction guide.
- A well thought out, documented process will help reduce and eliminate financial discrepancies and mistakes.
- There is a beginning and an end to every transaction.
- Know and understand every way you will conduct your business and record your transactions.
- Hold individuals that are responsible for each step in the process accountable.
- If the transaction process breaks down identify where the weakness exists and make corrections.
- The process to record and document each transaction must be thought out in advance with precise instructions on how to record it.

Step 8
Create Your Recordkeeping System

Create an organized, easy to understand record keeping system. It is essential in maintaining a good set of books and records.

1. Review the section in IRS publication 583 Starting a Business & Keeping Records.
   https://www.irs.gov/pub/irs-pdf/p583.pdf
2. Decide on a paperless or traditional file system.
3. Organize your file system into these categories:
   a. Permanent
   b. Tax return
   c. Payroll
      i. Employees
      ii. Tax payments & forms
      iii. Other
   d. Insurance
   e. Vendors
   f. Customers/Clients
   g. Other

Create Your Recordkeeping System

- IRS Publication 583 will provide detailed rules on record keeping.
- Your payroll, vendors and customer/client folders should be segregated by year and each document filed in chronological order.
- Your bookkeeping system includes your record keeping system.
- Your documents backup and verifies the transactions recorded in bookkeeping system.
- Your books and records must clearly reflect what is reported on your financial reports and tax returns.

Step 9
Paperless File Systems

Electronic file systems are the norm in today's business environment. The cost of printing, storing and handling paper documents is costly and vastly inefficient. Creating a virtual file cabinet with a strong naming convention will enable you to access any document in your system while still complying with recordkeeping requirements.

1. Choose your software for maintaining a paperless filing system. IE: Google Drive, Dropbox, etc.
2. Learn about the different file formats you can save electronic documents in. IE: PDF, XPS, etc.
3. Choose a scanner to convert your paper documents into electronic format.
4. Create your process for saving and maintaining your electronic documents.
5. Create a strong naming convention that will allow for quick retrieval.

Paperless File Systems

- There are 3 components to a paperless file system convention:
  - Format
  - Location
  - Naming
- Create a system that integrates with your bookkeeping system.
- Keep your electronic documents well organized.
- Your electronic file system should mirror your traditional file system.
- You will always have paper documents such as insurance policies, ownership titles, etc.
- Create an electronic version of any paper documents you still have to keep.

Step 10

Decide On Your Bookkeeping Platform

QuickBooks is the default choice for many small business owners but it is far from being the only choice. The most important factor is choosing the platform most appropriate for you and your business.

1. Working with your accountant decide on a platform that meets all of your bookkeeping objectives.
2. If you decide to use QuickBooks or any other software program obtain adequate training and support.
3. After implementing your system confirm that it is producing the desired results.

Decide On Your Bookkeeping Platform

- There are many bookkeeping software options in addition to QuickBooks.
- Check out www.waveapps.com
- Check out www.xero.com
- If you use any software obtain training and support.
- Most small businesses don't require complicated software.
- Select a platform that works for you.
- Sometimes a simple manual system will suffice.

Step 11
Recording Your Transactions

You record your transactions into lists that are called journals. A journal can be compared to a list detailing all of the transactions consummated during a monthly period and segregated by categories in chronological order.

1. Go back to step 2 item 2 for the list of transaction details needed.
2. If you use bookkeeping software such as QuickBooks your transactions are automatically posted to journals. Skip steps 3-8.
3. Invoices, purchases and payroll journals should be created if needed.
4. List each transaction in its corresponding journal in chronological order.
5. At the end of the month total each journal and make sure it adds across (Cross foots).

Recording Your Transactions

- Most small businesses will only need a cash receipts and cash disbursements journal.
- There is a journal for each of your business process cycles. Cash receipts, cash disbursements, payroll, sales, and purchases.
- If you are using computer software your journals are automatically created for you.
- Follow the software manufacturer's instructions on entering transactions in their software programs.

Step 12
Reconcile Your Accounts

The easiest way to verify that a transaction has been consummated and thus completed is to reconcile all of the accounts used in transacting business. This is a required process when maintaining accurate books and records.

1. Go to Youtube and do a search on How to do a bank reconciliation.
2. If you're using QuickBooks or other bookkeeping software follow the instructions provided by the software manufacturer.
3. Reconcile all of the accounts you transact business through including checking, credit cards and non-traditional accounts such as Paypal where you can receive and disburse money.
4. Identify all old, un-cleared transactions and determine if they need to be reversed.
5. Have your accountant review your bank and credit card reconciliations before they close your books and prepare your tax return.

Reconcile Your Accounts

- Reconciling verifies the dates and amounts of your transactions.
- Only cleared transactions should be reflected on your financial statements.
- Reconciling items should be reviewed for possible reversals, adjustments and corrections.
- Reconciliations' must be completed for all accounts business is consummated through including credit cards, PayPal, etc.

Step 13
Summarize Your Transactions

The next step is to take all of your journals and summarize them. This report is called a General Ledger. The totals from the GL balances are summarized into an Unadjusted Trial Balance. This is the report your accountant will use to create your financial reports.

1. Go online and search for examples of a trial balance and general ledger.
2. If you're using software such as QuickBooks the transactions are automatically posted to these reports.

Summarize Your Transactions

- The general ledger is a listing of the year to date transactions.
- A computer generated general ledger from a program such as QuickBooks may list all of the transactions in detail form.
- A manual General Ledger will show the monthly summary transactions posted from the individual journals.
- The trial balance is a list of the final totals of each General Ledger category and subcategory.

Step 14
Producing Meaningful Reports

By now you may be thinking that all of this seems so overwhelming and you want to throw in the towel. Don't fret because this is where a proactive accountant will come to your rescue. Broken down by steps bookkeeping is really very simple but even the most experienced bookkeepers' need the guidance of a good accountant. The best way to produce meaningful reports is with the assistance of your accountant.

1. Review step 3, your bookkeeping objectives.
2. Review your books and records with your accountant.
3. Have your accountant make any necessary adjustments to your trial balance.
4. With your accountants assistance produce your Balance Sheet and Income Statement.
5. If you are using software learn the procedures for producing those reports from the software help and/or training guides.

Producing Meaningful Reports

- Produce financial reports on a regular basis to measure the financial status of your business.
- Compare your year to date financial reports with the financial goals and objectives established earlier.

Step 15
Other Bookkeeping Considerations

There are many issues that can be traced back to your bookkeeping. Financial, payroll, payroll taxes, sales, tax compliance and everyday financial decisions require accurate, reliable, timely books and records. Bookkeeping should serve as the financial foundation of every business, big or small. Many business owners have made the mistake of treating bookkeeping as an afterthought, something that can be done later. The approach you take with your books and records will ripple throughout your entire business.

1. Take a responsible, informed approach to your bookkeeping.
2. Utilize the knowledge and experience your accountant provides.
3. Delegate segments of the bookkeeping process as appropriate.
4. Incorporate consistent review of your financial data.

Other Bookkeeping Considerations

- Bookkeeping is the financial foundation of your business.
- Utilize your accountant's' knowledge and experience to your advantage.
- The approach you take in building your bookkeeping system will ripple through your entire business.
- A solid bookkeeping system can help reduce and eliminate financial mistakes, fraud and theft.
- A solid bookkeeping foundation will help you make your business more profitable, easier to scale and sell.

You've finished. Before you go…

Tweet/share that you finished this book.

Please star rate this book.

Reviews are solid gold to writers. Please take a few minutes to give us some itty bitty feedback on this book and post it on the site from which you bought the book.

ABOUT THE AUTHOR

Joe DiChiara is an accomplished CPA, serial entrepreneur, speaker, author and business coach. He has worked with thousands of small businesses over his career and specializes in working with startups and small growing businesses.

In 2010 Mr. DiChiara began to develop a new philosophy for entrepreneurial success founded in the principles of "The Science of Getting Rich" by Wallace Wattles and "The Law of Success" by Napoleon Hill.

Through his latest enterprise Bedrock Business Builders, Joe teaches individuals virtually, a wide range of subjects from basic bookkeeping to starting and running a successful business.
His Definite Chief Aim is to help foster entrepreneurship around the globe and help people become rich.

BEDROCK
BUSINESS BUILDERS

www.bedrockbusinessbuilders.com

If you liked this Itty Bitty® Book You Might Also Enjoy

- **Your Amazing Itty Bitty® IRS Tax Audit Prevention Book** – Nellie Williams, EA
- **Your Amazing Itty Bitty® Business Tax Book** – Deborah A. Morgan, CPA
- **Your Amazing Itty Bitty® QuickBooks® Shortcuts Book – Barbara Starley, CPA**

Or our many other Amazing Itty Bitty® Books available online.

Made in the USA
Monee, IL
04 November 2026

67375736R00026